Word
Mastery
Primer

Printed with support from the Waldorf Curriculum Fund

Published by
Waldorf Publications at the
Research Institute for Waldorf Education
38 Main Street
Chatham, NY 12037

Title: *Word Mastery Primer for First and Second Graders*
Author: Hugh Renwick
Layout: Ann Erwin
Cover illustrations: "Vowel Sounds" by Natalie Simpson

© 2016 by Waldorf Publications
ISBN # 978-1-936367-87-0

Word Mastery Primer
for First and Second Graders

compiled by Hugh Renwick

Waldorf
PUBLICATIONS

RESEARCH INSTITUTE FOR Waldorf EDUCATION

Introduction

This primer has been compiled as an aid for teachers in Waldorf schools, and it may also be of value to others interested in the teaching of phonics in the early grades at any school or at home. I have, for the most part, followed the examples of three other phonetic primers in ordering the contents of this one: *Word Mastery* by Florence Akin (Riverside Press, Cambridge MA, 1913); *Reading with Phonics* by Julie Hay and Charles Wingo (J.B. Lippincott, Chicago, 1948); and *Why Johnny Can't Read* by Rudolph Flesch (Harper and Row, New York, 1966).

Our written language has developed historically from picture writing, a development which reflects a transformation in human consciousness that took place in earlier times. The growing child recapitulates in its development this and other transformations that humanity has passed through. For the first several years of his school life, the child's thinking mind is essentially pictorial. It is a basic principle of Waldorf education to teach reading and writing in a manner corresponding to this pictorial stage of the child's mental development.

Learning to read and write begins with the alphabet. If the letters of the alphabet are to be presented to children in a way that engages their picture-making minds, the letters should be given a concrete, pictorial character rather than an abstract one. The child will then be able to delight in each letter as it is learned, for he or she will be able to imagine in their forms the pictures of concrete things from the surrounding world and to associate a sound with the picture.

It is up to the teacher to imagine which pictures for the letters can best be used to give first graders a concrete and memorable experience of them. This is best done by telling stories which capture their imaginations, stories in which some thing or being is vividly described. The teacher can then show the children how each letter is derived from the form of such a thing or being. For example, the capital F can be derived from the form of a fish, the B from the form of a butterfly, the D from that of curved door, and so on, each presented in the context of a story.

Once this first step in reading development is taken, that is, once the children in first grade have seen and then drawn for themselves the pictorial origin of each letter which the teacher is free to imagine for and with them, they can then practice writing the abstract symbol which we grown ups now use for each letter, as well as writing simple words comprised of these symbols. As they do so, that symbol will not be an abstraction; it will have a concrete reference to a story and to a being or thing of importance in the story with a sound connected to it. Thus will their experience of learning to write and read the alphabetic letters and sounds be enlivened and more easily remembered.

This way of teaching the alphabet may seem suspect to someone concerned about historical accuracy. But that is not what is being aimed at or claimed. The point is to stimulate the child's imagination, pictorial thinking, and sense of sound which are natural at this age, and which make learning much more accessible and engaging.

In Waldorf schools the consonants and long vowels are usually taught early in the first grade in the manner described. The short vowels are taught later in the first grade year when the class is ready. The children need to be able to hear and distinguish the various short vowel sounds, and most can do so by the second half of first grade.

This primer is meant to aid in teaching the short vowel sounds and their combinations, as well as consonant blends, which will help children to develop their writing and reading skills. Its phonetic approach prepares children to read and spell by sounding out words. A phonetic ability gives children access to a very large set of words, including those they have never seen written before, and it strengthens their confidence in and enjoyment of reading.

This primer should be used in conjunction with lessons designed by the teacher. In Waldorf schools phonics lessons can be integrated with those main lesson blocks that deal with the language arts. They include the fairy tale blocks in first grade, the second grade animal-fable and saints blocks, the third grade Bible stories blocks, and the nature stories blocks in all three grades. Words can be taken from these stories in conjunction with the words listed in the primer which gradually increase in complexity. The primer can be used simply as a resource for teachers to take from as needed, or pages from it can be used as reading practice for the class or individual students. Some short animal stories have been included to serve as an introduction to printed readers. These stories fit well with themes from the first, second, and third grade main lessons.

Teaching the Long and Short Vowels

Here is a suggestion of a way it could be done. Beginning in the fall of first grade, the long vowels and their sounds can be derived from the form of five singing angels. For example, the long vowel sound *A* could be the name of the first angel and is the sound which she loves to sing, perhaps expressing a feeling and a gesture. Many teachers have developed an angel story around the Christmas theme and have taught the long vowels at that time in first grade, following upon the consonants earlier in the fall term. Up to this point, only capital letters are taught, written and read. By saving the short vowel forms and sounds for later in the year, the teacher can continue the story of the five angels; each angel, for instance, A has a little child, a, who can't yet sing the sound its parent can, but it can whisper the sound a bit differently:

> A sings the long *A* sound, but her little child, a, whispers *a* as in **a**pple.

> E sings long *E* sound, but her little child, e, whispers *e* as in **e**lephant.

> I sings long *I*, but i whispers i as in **I**ndian.

> O sings long O, but o whispers o as in **o**ctopus.

> U sings long *U*, but u whispers u as in **u**mbrella.

All of this should be part of a story which the teacher develops imaginatively for the children. As a result they will be fully engaged in learning. Once they have learned the lower case alphabet and the short vowel sounds, by the end of first grade, the children can sound them in short words, which begin and end with the various consonants. This Primer can be taken up at this point. It provides many lists of words which can facilitate progress in reading skill. (For example, many words contain vowels in combination—*coat, could*—which are more challenging to sound out and read. The Primer introduces these systematically.) The word lists can be first written by the teacher on the board for reading and writing practice. Some individual students may benefit from printed handouts of them, used in a tutorial context.

Some Exercises to Start

In first and second grades, the teacher can use various exercises to help the children discern the whispering or short vowel sounds in different words.

1. First reading exercises: Write short vowel words on the board and have children point to the vowels and sound them out. Draw word ladders on the board with a new word on each rung. One of the vowels stands alone on the bottom rung and words in which that vowel is present are placed on the rungs above. Start with monosyllabic words. Use the lower case letters whose forms you have already taught and the children have practiced writing. Have the children read up the ladders sounding the letters carefully. Examples below.

bat	bed	rib	pot	fun
cat	red	bib	not	bun
rat	fed	fib	lot	run
a	e	i	o	u

Start with monosyllabic words with the same last letter as above. Then vary the last letters on the ladders, using different words. Once you have covered the consonant blends like *ch, sh, nd, ck* (each one pictured as two friends playing together) and so on, then words with these blends can be practiced. All along, the children should practice writing these word ladders, either in their main lesson books or in word practice books. Once copied from the board, they can be read for practice in those books, in chorus or individually.

Ear exercises: Hold objects up for the class to see (fan, box, egg, and so forth) and have children sound the words slowly (phonetically): *f-a-n, b-o-x,* and so forth. Ask questions like: "Which whispering letter is in *run*?" By second grade, one can begin to call the vowels by their grown up names: long and short. "Which short vowel is in *cupcake*? Is there a long vowel too? What do you think makes it long?" (having taught the "silent e" rule).

Dictation exercises: Each child can have a small slate at his desk for writing the lists, which can be part of the warm-up exercises to begin each day in the early grades. Children can copy from the board, and then, as they become more adept, write from dictation.

Memory training: Beginning in second grade, a special list of memory words can be posted each week for practice. Such words could include vowel blends in which only one vowel is sounded: "When two vowels go walking, the first does the talking." Examples include words such as *each, reach, boat, coat,* and so forth, and words ending with *-tion,* like *action* and *mention.* Such words are not strictly phonetic in spelling because they contain unsounded letters. They simply need to be memorized. The Primer includes lots of examples. The following circle spelling exercises can help with memorization.

5. Circle Spelling Exercises: Practice spelling words out loud in chorus, as the class walks in a circle on the floor, each step a letter in each word, forwards, then backward. Work through a spelling list for each week, stepping and spelling each word, then standing still on the circle and spelling out loud; then standing still and spelling silently in heads; then on the last day of the week include an additional step: going back to desks and writing the words – from dictation. Such movement exercises culminating in silent, "inner" spelling can strengthen spelling ability and make the writing of words and sentences from dictation much easier. The teacher can lead them from second through fourth or fifth grade; a little bit each day goes a long way.

The phonetic approach to writing, spelling, and reading which this primer makes possible will strengthen children's ability in these activities. If teachers do not spend sufficient time with phonetic instruction and practice, reading and spelling skills may suffer. Thus, in reading, children may skip over longer words they don't recognize or simply guess at them as they lack practice in sounding them out. Although in spelling, children will usually be able to remember the first and last letters of longer words, what comes in between may often be muddled and confused. Step by step learning of consonant and vowel sounds, alone and in their various combinations, as well as daily and weekly writing and reading practice, are essential to prevent such outcomes.

Table of Contents

Review the Consonant Sounds

B	b	P	p
C	c	Q	q
D	d	R	r
F	f	S	s
G	g	T	t
H	h	V	v
J	j	W	w
K	k	X	x
L	l	Y	y
M	m	Z	z
N	n		

Read the Consonants

b	q
g	v
k	f
l	g
m	r
n	l
t	j
p	n
r	m
t	c
s	x
d	w
b	z
p	b

Whispering Vowels (short vowels)

a

a

at

cat

bat

hat

sat

mat

pat

rat

a

an

can

fan

man

pan

ran

tan

ban

e

e	**e**
net	Ned
pet	Ted
get	bed
let	fed
wet	red
set	wed
met	led

i

i	i
it	in
bit	pin
hit	tin
sit	sin
wit	win
fit	fin
pit	kin
mit	bin

o

o	**o**
dot	hop
hot	mop
lot	pop
pot	top
cot	lop
tot	sop
not	bop
got	cop

u

<u>u</u>	<u>u</u>	<u>u</u>
cut	sun	cup
nut	gun	pup
but	run	sup
rut	fun	
hut	bun	
mut		

a	**e**	**i**
cap	wed	hid
lap	red	did
map	led	lid
nap	fed	bid
gap	bed	kid
sap	Ned	rid
tap	hem	dip
bad	beg	hip
had	leg	lip
mad	peg	rip
sad	web	tip
pad	vex	sip

o	**u**	**a**
pod	bud	am
rod	mud	jam
nod	gum	ham
sod	hum	Sam
hog	bug	tag
log	rug	bag
fog	hug	rag
cob	jug	sag
rob	pug	cab
mob	tug	ax
ox	tub	wax
box	rub	tax

Alphabetic Review

an	cat	fan
at	cap	fat
am	cob	fed
ax	cot	fig
	cub	fin
bat	cup	fit
bad		fog
bag	Dan	fox
bed	den	fun
big	did	
bit	dig	gas
box	dim	get
bug	dot	got
	din	gum
cab	dug	gun

hat	jam	men
had	jet	met
hen	jug	mix
hid		mud
him	keg	
hop		nap
hog	lap	net
hot	let	not
hug	lip	nod
hum	log	nut
hut	lug	
		on
if	man	ox
it	map	
in	mat	pan

pet	set	up
pig	sit	us
pin	six	
pod	sob	van
pop	sun	vex
pug		
	tag	wax
rag	tag	web
red	tax	web
rim	tap	wig
rob	ten	win
rug	tin	
	top	yes
sad	tub	yet
set	tug	zig zag

General Review

can	let	tip
bit	pat	sad
ham	Tom	wax
let	beg	peg
Dan	rug	mix
lip	Nan	tub
rod	rap	box
beg	map	log
fed	bed	cab
sit	fig	hem
did	rob	red
tag	vex	big
lid	jug	keg

Whispering and Singing Vowels

at	can	Sam
ate	cane	same
hat	pan	mad
hate	pane	made
mat	man	fad
mate	mane	fade
rat	cap	hid
rate	cape	hide
fat	tap	dim
fate	tape	dime

fin	bit	not
fine	bite	note
pin	rid	cut
pine	ride	cute
tin	rod	us
tine	rode	use
win	hop	tub
wine	hope	tube
din	mop	cub
dine	mope	cube
rip	lop	
ripe	lope	

Singing Vowels

wade	case	life
safe	vase	wife
bake	Kate	mile
make	date	pile
take	gate	tile
gale	gave	lime
sale	save	time
tale	wave	mine
came	gaze	line
game		nine
name		wipe
Jane		like
lane		fire

fire	cone	tune
five	tone	June
hive	lone	Luke
dive	rope	Duke
live	home	pure
	dome	cure
poke	tore	mule
joke	wore	mute
yoke	more	
pole	dose	he
hole		be
mole	no	we
sole	go	me
bone	so	

Review

late	hive	home
mine	mane	cape
gave	rate	date
bite	tine	robe
pole	yoke	Duke
cane	pane	dive
wire	pile	fade
dime	more	gate
hope	ride	rode
pure	tire	vane
wore	pipe	hire
line	lake	ate
bone	pine	June
rake	ripe	cake

core	wake	hole
kite	Kate	tame
make	side	wine
same	lame	Luke
safe	note	tape
vine	Jane	wipe
sale	cure	bale
pale	wave	mule
vote	size	pave
sake	use	name
made	nine	bake
lone	mate	here
wade	cave	came
case	take	tune

S at the End of Words

cat	cake	rakes
cats	cakes	rats
cap	gate	makes
caps	gates	wipes
sit	pipe	jokes
sits	pipes	bakes
dip	bite	tips
dips	bites	dates
top	rope	cups
tops	ropes	wakes
nut	yoke	kites
nuts	yokes	wets

S = Z

as	games	boxes
has	tunes	sixes
is	rose	hose
his	roses	wise
pins	nose	rise
lids	noses	rises
rugs	axes	mixes
	taxes	fuse

The Possessive: 's

Ned's cap Ben's cup

Kate's rose Sam's bat

Tom's cane Ted's dime

Jane's cake mule's rope

Dan's fox cat's bed

Dave's home hen's leg

Nat's box man's gun

Bob's top pig's pen

Consonant Blends: Word Endings

ck	**ll**	**ss**
back	bell	mass
pack	fell	pass
deck	sell	less
neck	well	hiss
pick	ill	kiss
lick	bill	fuss
kick	fill	muss
sick	hill	**ff**
lock	kill	ruff
rock	mill	puff
buck	will	**zz**
duck	doll	fuzz
luck	dull	buzz

Review

left	send	hand
huff	tilt	sift
hemp	hint	lend
went	west	hiss
less	romp	held
Jack	mess	add
Jill	wick	bell
next	pump	dent
mock	pick	Bill

ch

ch	**ch**	**tch**
chair	such	patch
chick	much	latch
choke	rich	catch
chin	bench	hatch
chime	lunch	match
chase	bunch	itch
check	punch	witch
chill		pitch
chafe	**ch = k**	hitch
chip	Christmas	ditch

sh

sh	**sh**	**shr**
shell	ash	shrub
shake	cash	shrill
shall	dash	shrimp
shame	lash	shred
shape	mash	shrug
shed	sash	
shelf	dish	
shine	wish	
ship	fish	
shock	hush	

th

th	**thr**	**th**
thin	thrill	with
thump	throb	width
the	thrive	tenth
that	throne	
then	thrash	bathe
this	thrush	
these	thrust	
those	thrift	
them		
thus		
thimble		

wh

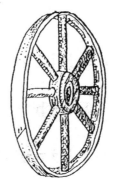

wh	**wh**
wheel	wheat
whip	whiff
whale	while
when	whack
whet	white
which	whim
whine	whiz

I saw a big _____ _____ .

Review

shake	chill	shuck
thatch	mush	chop
chores	whine	then
which	with	chest
shift	shade	thrush
this	these	shrill
shape	the	match
chase	whiz	witch
ship	chin	those
throne	hush	while

Consonant Blends: Word Beginnings

bl

cl

fl

bl	cl	fl
black	clam	flag
blade	clap	flake
blame	click	flame
bled	clip	flat
bless	clod	flesh
block	close	flit
blot	close	flock
bluff	clove	flop
blunt	club	flume

gl	**sp**	**sl**
glad	spade	slack
glade	span	slab
glaze	speck	slash
glide	spell	sled
globe	spill	slave
	spine	slip
pl	spoke	slid
plan	spot	slit
plate	spun	slim
plume	spike	slope
plush	splash	slug

gr	**tr**	**st**
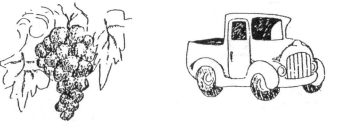		
grape	truck	stack
grade	track	stab
graze	tramp	stake
grate	trash	stamp
grip	trap	state
grill	trade	step
grin	trick	stem
grove	trip	stick
grunt	trot	stiff
pr	trod	stove
press	**spr**	stole
pride	sprig	stuff
prize	sprite	stub

br	**cr**	**sk**

bran	crab	skate
brag	crack	sketch
brave	crate	skill
brick	cramp	skin
brim	crept	skip
brine	crisp	skim
broke	crush	
brush	crust	

sc	**dr**	**fr**

sc	dr	fr
scales	drag	frame
scamp	drape	fret
scat	dress	fresh
scant	drift	French
score	drill	frill
scum	drive	frock
scr	drop	from
scrap	drove	frog
scrape	drug	frisk
scratch	drum	froze
scrub	drip	

sm	**sn**	**qu**
smash	snake	quack
smack	snap	quill
smell	snatch	quilt
smith	sniff	quit
smile	snipe	quite
smoke	snore	quiz
smug	snug	quick
sw	**tw**	squint
swam	twig	
swell	twill	
swim	twine	
switch	twin	

Review

blend	crust	clamp
squint	trade	sprig
stripe	frame	scrape
broke	twist	risk
fleck	spend	flap
slide	grim	snatch
stitch	quench	scamp
drape	fluff	splash
smile	skate	swift
print	swan	clump

The y Sounds

y	y = long e	y = long i
yak	candy	by
Yale	carry	my
yell	cherry	cry
yelp	merry	dry
yet	penny	fly
yes	twenty	fry
yoke	chilly	pry
	sixty	sly
	fifty	spy
	copy	try
	sorry	shy
	dusty	why
	funny	style

Vowel Digraphs

ai = long a

aid	tail
laid	trail
maid	aim
paid	claim
braid	gain
ail	rain
fail	drain
bail	brain
rail	grain
hail	train
jail	strain
mail	sprain
nail	main

ay = long a

bay
day
ray
tray
gay
gray
hay
lay
clay
may
pay
play
say

ea = long e

sea	weak	lean
tea	streak	mean
flea	sneak	clean
each	squeak	heap
beach	heal	leap
peach	meal	cheap
reach	seal	reap
teach	squeal	ear
bead	steal	fear
lead	beam	hear
read	seam	near
leaf	team	tear
leak	steam	dear
beak	stream	year

ee = long e

see	beef	sheen
bee	reef	deep
flee	seek	keep
free	week	sheep
glee	cheek	sweep
three	creek	sleep
tree	meek	deer
speech	eel	cheer
screech	feel	queer
deed	heel	beet
feed	steel	feet
need	seem	sheet
seed	screen	sweet
weed	queen	street

oa = long o

load	loan
road	moan
toad	soap
loaf	oat
coach	coat
poach	float
roach	goat
oak	boat
cloak	throat
croak	oar
soak	soar
coal	roar
goal	board
foam	coarse

oe = long o

toe

woe

hoe

foe

ue = long u

sue

cue

hue

due

Review

merry	yes	why
braid	each	hay
week	road	sleep
rain	east	toad
penny	sly	play
chilly	float	braid
fail	gray	shy
beach	chilly	cry
play	sweep	year
team	hear	deer
oak	goat	throat
croak	coal	soap

Word Endings: *-ing, -ings*

king	running	singing
kings	boxing	bringing
ring	rubbing	fretting
rings	rubbings	braiding
sing	mixing	playing
sings	packing	reading
string	puffing	meeting
strings	buzzing	meetings
sling	hissing	spitting
wings	bending	loaning
swing	hunting	lifting
spring	resting	rolling
bring	jumping	trying
thing	helping	staying

Word Endings: -er, -ers

her	rubber	cracker
were	deeper	crackers
jerk	temper	Easter
nerve	pitcher	miller
perch	hammer	grinder
fern	timber	sleeper
verse	roller	teacher
ever	thunder	sifter
stern	older	bitter
term	brother	mother
sister	colder	father
flower	dinner	grandfather

The Little White Cat

One chilly day a little white cat lay asleep on the grass. The wind blew a big gust and woke up the cat. A girl with a braid in her hair came by. She had a black dog with her that was tied to a rope.

When the dog saw the cat, he jumped at her. The girl held on to the rope until it broke. The big dog went after the cat as fast as a shot from a gun.

The little cat ran faster than the dog did. She jumped up into a tree. She hissed and she spat at the dog from a branch of the tree.

"Go away, you silly dog," hissed the cat. "You can never catch me."

The big dog barked and barked at her. "Come here, Fluffy, and play with me," he said.

The cat stopped hissing and spitting. "I do not want to play with such a bully as you," the cat said.

"I will not be a bully," the dog said. "Come and play with me and you will see."

"Well," said the cat, "I will only play with you if you let me chase you. Why don't you run away from me, and then I will chase you?"

The dog smiled and said, "Yes, Fluffy, I will run and you can chase me."

The dog did not tell the cat what he was thinking. "I will trick this little cat. When she chases me, I will turn and catch her before she can get away!"

So the dog ran off. The girl with the braid in her hair followed him.

The little white cat did not move. She stayed in the tree. "I am glad to be rid of that silly dog," she said. "Now I can go back to sleep."

In a little while the dog stopped running. He turned and saw that the cat was not there. "What has become of that little white cat?" he asked.

Just then the girl with the braid in her hair ran up to the dog. She tied the rope to his collar. "Come, Jeb," she said. "It's time for us to go home."

The Long *i* and Long *o*

long i	igh = long i
mild	sigh
wild	fight
child	might
bind	high
blind	light
find	night
hind	right
kind	tight
mind	bright
wind	flight
grind	sight

long o

old	told
cold	gold
hold	bold
mold	sold
scold	roll
stroll	post
most	colt
jolt	pork
pork	worn
porch	both
toll	forth

ow = long o

owe	grown
bow	flown
low	thrown
blow	blown
flow	growth
row	yellow
grow	window
glow	elbow
mow	hollow
crow	shadow
show	**ou = long o**
snow	four
throw	pour
stow	court

The *ow* Sound as in *Owl*

ow	ou = ow	
owl	couch	mount
howl	crouch	our
fowl	pouch	sour
scowl	slouch	scour
growl	loud	flour
bow	cloud	house
brow	proud	mouse
cow	bound	grouse
how	found	blouse
now	mound	out

When *o* and *ou* Sound Like Short *u*

o = short u		ou = short u
son	dove	young
won	love	younger
wonder	gloves	wondrous
none	front	serious
done	month	touched
some	nothing	trouble
somebody	color	double
something	colored	country
somewhere	comfort	couple
come	other	
mother	another	

When *ph* and *gh* Sound Like *f*

ph = f	gh = f
Philip	cough
Ralph	coughing
telephone	trough
telegraph	rough
photograph	roughest
phonics	tough
Joseph	toughen
orphan	enough
nephew	laugh
elephant	laughing
alphabet	laughter

Review

child	kind	bright
light	bold	both
cold	flow	row
stroll	shadow	four
owe	crouch	house
owl	cloud	out
son	dove	touched
wonder	front	double
telephone	elephant	laugh
cough	wagon	circus
animal	near	hear
clown	always	story

Queen, the Elephant

Once there was an elephant called Queen. She lived in a circus. Queen was not the only elephant in the circus, but she was the biggest elephant.

The circus animals lived in cages on top of the wagons. Each wagon must be put in its place. That was Queen's job. The wagons were light and easy for her to move. All but one wagon.

There was one wagon that Queen never wanted to go near. It was a big wagon. In that wagon was a rhinoceros. A rhinoceros is a very big and dangerous animal. A rhinoceros will attack any animal, even a big elephant. Queen never went near that rhinoceros.

In the circus Queen and a clown always made the people laugh. The clown would take Queen's trunk and talk into it just as if he were talking into a telephone.

As soon as the clown had "talked into the telephone," Queen would turn around. Then the clown would take Queen's tail and hold it to his ear just as if he were using a telephone. The clown would laugh and laugh just as if he were hearing something very funny over the telephone.

The people at the circus always laughed at Queen and the clown.

After many years the clown left the circus. He went to live in a big city. But if a circus came to the city, the clown always went to see it.

One day the clown went to a circus. He was not dressed as a clown now. He was standing near the elephants talking to some people. Someone was telling the clown a funny story. The clown was laughing and laughing.

All at once, one of the elephants began to stamp her feet. The men could not get the elephant to be still. The clown went over to see what was the matter.

It was Queen who was making all the fuss. She had seen it was her clown. And the clown saw what to do. He took Queen's trunk and talked into it just as if it were a telephone. Then the big elephant turned around. The clown took the elephant's tail and put it to his ear just as if he were using a telephone.

Queen was happy to see her clown again.
But the funny thing was that the elephant
had not seen her clown for twenty years.

General Review

flesh	blade	Jack's
bone	socks	leader
shift	spins	snake
supper	mopping	froth
trust	stretch	post
sorrow	sand	whiz
perch	peach	cores
off	patter	thrush
four	glad	stand
suppose	clinch	plump
clings	bench	twine
greedy	weaker	blister
cloth	offer	June
follow	scolding	shelf
slope	smile	twelfth

feeds	toss	dray
stake	study	oaks
cheese	splash	frills
times	street	coats
swept	shadow	cherry
check	trout	saves
trench	crust	frosty
ever	vote	feelers
fish	stitch	lamp
shells	kind	preach
bluff	twig	sleeve
sniffs	clerk	toast
tried	sweets	crown

Word Endings: *-ang, -ong, -ung, -ength*

bang	song	sung
hang	songs	stung
hanger	gong	swung
rang	prong	slung
gang	strong	sprung
gangway	tongs	strung
clang	hung	length
sprang	rung	strength

n = ng

bank	thanking	think
blank	drank	blink
clank	tank	sunk
plank	ink	chunk
rank	link	trunk
crank	mink	trunks
Frank	pink	hunger
thank	sink	angry

Drop the e and Add -ing

make	raise	trade
making	raising	trading
skate	close	stroke
skating	closing	stroking
wave	freeze	blame
waving	freezing	blaming
hide	squeeze	whine
hiding	squeezing	whining
smile	please	choke
smiling	pleasing	choking
stone	leave	chase
stoning	leaving	chasing
hope	weave	tame
hoping	weaving	taming

Silent Letters: *k, w, b, g*

kn = n	**wr = r**	**mb = m**
knob	wrap	lamb
knot	wraps	lambskin
knee	wren	limb
kneel	wrench	comb
knit	wring	climb
knife	wringing	dumb
know	wrist	crumb
knows	wrong	numb
knight	write	plumbing
knead	writes	**gn = n**
knack	writing	gnat
knock	wrote	gnash
knocking	wreck	sign

More Silent Letters

gu = g

guess

guesses

guide

guest

bu = b

build

builds

builder

buy

bt = t

doubt

doubts

doubting

debt

gue = g

plague

rogue

league

leagues

mn = m

hymn

autumn

solemn

lf = f

calf

calves

half

halves

lm = m

calm

palm

Word Endings: *-ed*

petted	crowded	waded
landed	sifted	seated
faded	folded	pouted
tested	clouded	roasted
needed	boasted	handed
twisted	tended	doubted
wicked	rented	coasted
tinted	jolted	mended

ed = d

sailed	peeled	buttered
played	frowned	roared
kneeled	foamed	wheeled
plowed	breathed	shivered
aimed	pinned	cleaned
loaned	prayed	snowed

ed = t

reached	wrecked	kissed
puffed	liked	guessed
baked	wrapped	dropped
clapped	stamped	coaxed
ticked	leaped	checked
brushed	dressed	shipped
patched	knocked	scraped

The Deer and the Lion

Once upon a time there was a big lion who was very strong. Every day he killed many animals in the forest.

One day all the animals in the forest came to the lion and said, "King Lion, we know that you are very strong. We know that every day you kill many animals. Every day you kill animals that you do not eat."

The lion roared and said, "I am the king of animals, and I am stronger than any of you. What are you going to do about it?"

Then an old deer said, "We have been thinking. We will send one animal to you every day. You can eat that animal and all of us will live a bit longer."

"That is fine," roared the lion. "I will not work at all. I will sit in the sun and sleep. But see to it that an animal comes every day, for I must eat to stay healthy."

The oldest fox came to the lion, and King Lion ate the fox. And then the lion ran and played, and when he was tired, he went to sleep in the sun.

And the day after that day, the oldest bear came to the lion. And the lion ate the bear.

And the day after that day, it was time for the oldest deer to go to the lion.

The oldest deer had lived a long time and he knew many things. He did not want the lion to kill him. He did not walk very fast to where the lion lived. And he stopped at a big well for a long time and gazed into the water. Then he said to himself, "Now I know what I shall tell the lion."

When the lion saw the oldest deer, he roared, "You take too long to come to me. I have had nothing to eat all day, and I want to eat you right now."

"I saw another lion in the forest," said the oldest deer. "He was going to eat me. I told him that I had to go to the King of the Lions. Only the biggest and strongest lion in the forest may eat me. But it was a long time before this lion let me go."

"What?" roared the King of Lions. "You say that there is another lion in the forest?"

"Yes," said the oldest deer, "and he is a very big lion. I guess he is even bigger than you."

"Take me to him," roared the King of Lions. "I will kill him at once, for I will not have another lion in my forest."

And so the oldest deer showed King lion the big well. The lion looked into the water in the well. "There is another lion down there," roared the King of Lions. And he jumped into the well.

Down into the water went the King of Lions. He was not able to get out of the well. And so that was the end of the King of Lions.

More Vowel Digraphs

ea = long a

break

breaks

braker

breaking

daybreak

greater

steak

beefsteak

ea = short e

head	dead
read	dread
ready	dread
lead	bread
spread	thread
deaf	breast
breast	health
feather	healthy
weather	

ie = long e   ai = short e

ie = long e	ai = short e
chief	captain
thief	fountain
thieves	mountain
brief	
field	
priest	
wield	
yield	
shield	
grief	
grieve	

The Double Consonant Rule

mating	pining	holy
matting	pinning	holly
loping	diner	later
lopping	dinner	latter
filing	moping	hoping
filling	mopping	hopping
sloping	shaming	bating
slopping	shamming	batting

---

happy	planning	blotter
ladder	supper	cracker
bonnet	yellow	rabbit
summer	begging	carry

More Vowel Digraphs

ei = long a	eigh = long a	ey = long a
skein	eight	they
reins	eighteen	grey
reindeer	eighty	greyhound
veil	eighty-five	whey
vein	weigh	prey
	weight	
	neigh	
	freight	

The Long *oo* Sound as in *boot*

boost	gloom	loose
hoof	gloomy	broom
roof	soon	root
proof	moon	hoot
cool	noon	shoot
pool	spoon	boost
tool	teaspoon	choose
stool	loop	coo
spool	looped	coop
food	droop	scoop
room	stoop	scooped
boom	hoop	groove
bloom	goose	poor

Words that Sound Like *oo*

do	truth	whoop
to	soup	who
move	croup	who
prove	group	whom
shoe	grouped	whose
shoemaker	fruit	
tomb	bruise	**ew = long u**
blue	gruised	mew
glue	cruise	new
true	drew	few
rude	grew	dew
ruby	crew	stew
rubies	screw	
rule	strew	

The Short *oo* Sound as in *book*

good	wood	look
good-bye	woodpile	looked
hood	woodshed	brook
childhood	cook	brooks
stood	cooking	crooked
understood	hook	foot
took	fishhook	wool
undertook	shook	wolf
		wolves

Words that Sound like Short *oo*

could	**<u>-ful</u>**
should	cheerful
would	thankful
put	dreadful
putting	powerful
puss	tearful
push	spiteful
bush	helpful
bushes	truthful
butcher	painful
pudding	fretful
pull	frightful
full	bashful

The *oi* and *oy* Sound

oil	toy
toil	Roy
soil	boy
boil	joy
spoil	enjoy
coin	enjoyment
join	joyful
joint	oyster
point	boyhood
moist	
noise	
noisy	

Review

vein	boot	book
reins	room	took
reindeer	shoot	wolf
they	shoe	put
eight	who	push
eighteen	blue	should
weigh	fruit	could
weight	true	cheerful
greyhound	soup	grateful
noise	enjoyment	point

The Goat and the Wolf

Once upon a time there were seven goats who lived on a farm together. Every morning the farmer let the goats out and they went up on the hills and ate grass. A big black dog went with them. He looked after the goats.

At night the big black dog led the goats down from the hills. The goats went back to the farm and the farmer put them into the barn.

But one night one of the goats did not go down from the hills with the other goats. He went up the hill so that the big black dog could not find him. And he said to himself, "I have always wanted to sleep up in the hills all night. And so I will not go back to the barn tonight."

The goat was very glad to get away from the big black dog so that he could sleep up in the hills at night. But he did not see a hungry old wolf that had come to the hills looking for someting to eat.

"Brother Goat," said the wolf, "what are you doing on my hills at night?"

Now the goat thought very fast and so he said to the wolf, "Brother Wolf, I was just looking for you. I wanted to thank you for the green grass that grows upon your hills."

"Don't you know that I like to eat a goat," said the wolf.

"Oh, yes," said the goat. "I know that you are going to eat me. But all this time I have been eating the green grass that grows on your hills. And now it is only right that you should eat me."

The wolf thought that was a very funny thing for a goat to say. The goat went on, "Brother Wolf, I have one thing to ask of you before you eat me."

"And what is that?" asked the wolf.

"I want to sing before you eat me," said the goat.

"'I did not know that you could sing," said the wolf.

"Oh, yes," said the goat. "I am a very good singer. And I always like to sing the last thing at night before I go to sleep."

Now the wolf thought that this was a very funny goat. And so he said, "Brother

Goat, sing to me, for I have never heard a goat sing."

And so the goat put back his head and called "B-a-a, b-a-a."

"I think that is very funny," said the wolf. "Is that all that you can sing?"

"Oh, no," said the goat. "I have more to sing."

And the goat put back his head and called, "B-a-a, b-a-a, b-a-a."

The big black dog heard the goat calling. he ran up the hill as fast as he could go. And he found the goat.

The wolf saw the dog coming and he ran away. He did not get a goat to eat that night.

Word Endings: *-le, -tle*

le = l

apple

cattle

saddle

tumble

candle

thimble

steeple

cuddle

puddle

tinkle

pickle

tle = l

kettle

maple

bottle

beetle

cradle

wiggle

handle

eagle

tremble

bundle

brittle

thistle

wrestle

whistle

bristle

nestle

rustle

trestle

c = s before *e*, *i* and *y*

ce = s

ice	fence	
rice	quince	
mice	since	
nice	Prince	
slice	Alice	
price	ounce	
twice	bounce	
face	flounce	
lace	cell	
place	center	
space	cease	
grace	piece	

cy = s

juicy

spicy

cyclone

bicycle

Lucy

ci = s

pencil

city

cider

cinders

g = j before *e, i* and *y*

ge = j	**gi = j**	**dg = j**
gem	engine	badge
age	ginger	edge
stage	gingerbread	ledge
range		hedge
change	**gy = j**	ridge
strange	dingy	bridge
danger	Egypt	dodge
gentle	gypsy	budge
huge		nudge
page		judge
college		pledge

Word Endings: *-ly, -less*

-ly

safely	likely	
gaily	daily	
fully	badly	
sadly	freely	
gladly	swiftly	
lightly	quickly	
slowly	gently	
poorly	kindly	
loudly	lately	
slyly	truly	
nicely	bravely	
softly	neatly	

-less

blameless
aimless
useless
homeless
fearless
tasteless
tireless
lifeless
painless
endless
boundless
priceless

Word Endings: *-ness, -est*

sweetness	coldest	dampest
kindness	nicest	sorest
meanness	loudest	stiffest
illness	lightest	wisest
stillness	slowest	latest
thickness	kindest	finest
weakness	tamest	lowest
loneliness	safest	oldest
happiness	tightest	widest
sadness	ripest	dearest
sickness	wildest	brightest
goodness	sweetness	happiest

Review

thistle	strange	kindness
price	greatest	engine
bounce	bridge	widest
tallest	first	brightest
cease	ridge	oldest
twice	safely	whistle
bottle	juicy	happiness
cider	nicely	looking
center	twenty	fight
eats	leaves	kicking
danger	mother	animal
everything	endless	bicycle
eagle	change	swiftly

The Ape and the Firefly

The ape is the very biggest of the monkeys. He is very big compared to the lovely firefly.

One night an ape was looking at the fireflies flying cheerfully about. They were lighting their little, bright lights and then putting them out, and then lighting them again and then putting them out.

The fireflies looked very pretty. And the ape thought he would have fun with them. So he said to the biggest firefly, "Mr. Firefly, I would like you to tell me why you always carry a light."

"I show my light so the mosquitoes will not hurt me," said the firefly.

"Ho, ho," laughed the ape. "You are afraid of the mosquitoes."

"I am not afraid of the mosquitoes," said the firefly. "I show my light because I do not want the mosquitoes to hurt me."

"You are a coward," said the ape, "because you are afraid of the mosquitoes."

"I am not a coward," said the firefly.

The ape laughed at the firefly. And he said to the other apes that the firefly was a coward because he was afraid of the mosquitoes.

"I will show you that I am not a coward," said the firefly. "Will you fight with me tomorrow night?"

The big ape laughed. And all the other apes laughed. It was very, very funny that a firefly wanted to fight an ape. "You had better bring all the other fireflies to help you," said the ape. And I will bring some other apes to help me kill you, Mr. Firefly!"

"Bring as many apes with you as you want," said the firefly. "Tomorrow night I will show you that I am no coward."

The next night ten big apes came. And each ape had a big stick. "Do you want to fight?" asked the big ape.

"Yes," said the firefly "I do. And I shall show you that I am not a coward."

"Where are the other fireflies that are going to help you?" said the big ape.

"The other fireflies are watching from the trees," said the firefly. "They do not have to help me fight the apes."

The firefly sat upon the big ape's nose. The next ape tried to hit the firefly with his stick. But the firefly jumped and the stick came down on the big ape's nose. The ape cried out for his nose hurt very badly. He ran away into the woods.

Then the firefly showed his light. He sat down on another ape's nose. Another ape tried to hit the firefly with his stick. But the firefly jumped and the stick came down on the ape's nose. That ape ran away into the woods.

And so it was. The firefly showed his light and sat on an ape's nose. Another ape tried to hit the firefly with his stick. But the firefly jumped and the stick came down on the ape's nose. In no time at all, all the apes were running into the woods, crying loudly because their noses were hurting so badly.

Then all the fireflies came out of the trees and showed their lights. They laughed and laughed at the apes. They called after the apes, "Never again say that a firefly is a coward!"

Now when night comes and the fireflies show their lights, the apes run away into the woods. No ape wants a firefly to sit upon his nose.

The *er* Sound

er	**ir = er**	**ear = er**
lantern	bird	earn
desert	chirp	learn
finger	girl	earth
rooster	first	search
every	skirt	heard
flutter	birthday	
spider	squirrel	
	third	
ar = er	dirt	
beggar		
cedar		
dollar		
backward		

or = er	**ur = er**
word	bur
work	fur
world	blur
worm	sturdy
worse	curl
worst	purse
stubborn	burn
flavor	hurt
tailor	purple
doctor	church
neighbor	turtle
	further

The *ar* Sound as in *Star*

yard	darkness	art
bar	mark	artist
marble	parlor	tart
arch	spark	cart
car	sparkle	dart
scar	lark	part
starch	arm	start
starve	farm	charge
hard	harm	
bark	harmless	
dark	charm	
star	barn	

The *air* Sound as in *Chair*

<u>air</u>	**<u>are = air</u>**	**<u>ear = air</u>**
chair	care	bear
airy	carefully	pear
fair	careless	tear
fairy	dare	tearing
fairest	daring	wear
hair	barefoot	
hairbrush	hare	**<u>eir = air</u>**
pair	spare	their
stair	square	
staircase	rarely	**<u>ere = air</u>**
	hardware	there
	glare	where
	snare	nowhere

The *aw* Sound as in *Saw*

	al = aw	**ough = aw**
jaw	all	ought
gnaw	almost	bought
law	ball	brought
claw	call	fought
paw	fall	sought
hawk	salt	thought
draw	walk	nought
strawberry	sidewalk	
thaw	talk	
yawn	chalk	
scrawl		
dawn		
sawn		

When *ti* Sounds like *sh*

ti = sh

vacation

action

collection

station

nation

combination

relation

recitation

motion

attention

addition

invitation

ci = sh

musician

physician

precious

delicious

special

ce = sh

ocean

Review

saw	all	thought
lantern	bird	learn
every	first	earth
word	fur	hurt
doctor	curl	purple
star	darkness	artist
starve	farm	cart
chair	care	tear
hairbrush	carefully	bear
where	there	ought
east	their	brought
walking	north	laughing

The Bear Says North

One day a big old bear got hold of a bird. He had the bird in his mouth and he thought.

"Just see what I have done. I wish everyone in the woods could see me now. They think that I am a funny old bear. They are always laughing at me. They do not think that I could get hold of a bird like this."

Just then a fox came by. He saw the bear with the bird in his mouth. And the fox thought, "That funny old bear is very much pleased that he got hold of a bird. I think that I will fool him.

The fox walked up to the bear and said, "I have been walking in the woods all morning. But I cannot tell from which way the wind is coming. Mr. Bear, which way is the wind coming from?"

The bear said, "Um, um, um, "because he wanted the fox to see the bird he had in his mount.

But the fox said, "Mr. Bear, did you say that the wind was coming from the south?"

"Um, um, um," said the bear because that was all he could say with the bird in his mouth.

"Oh," said the fox, "you do not think that the wind is coming from the south."

"Um, um, um," said the bear.

"Well," said the fox, "if you do not think that the wind is from the south, tell me, Mr. Bear, from which way do you think the wind is coming?"

The bear opened his mouth and said, "North." As soon as the bear opened his mouth, the bird flew away.

The fox laughed and laughed.

"Just look what you made me do," said the bear. "I wanted to show everyone how I had got hold of a bird."

"I did not make you do anything," said the fox.

"You asked me which way the wind was blowing," said the bear. "I opened my mouth and said, 'North,' and the bird flew away."

"But why did you open your mouth?" asked the fox.

"You cannot say 'North' if you do not open your mouth," said the bear.

"Well," said the fox. "If I had a bird in my mouth and you asked me about the wind, I would not have said, 'North'."

"What would you have said?" asked the bear.

The fox laughed and laughed. Then he put his teeth together and said, "East."

Review Vowel Sounds

bail	lag	lap	rib	rack
bile	leg	lip	rob	rock
boil	log	loop	robe	rake
bale	lug	leap	rub	reek

reel	sad	spark	top	veal
rail	side	speak	tap	vile
rill	sod	spook	tip	vale
roll	seed	spike	tape	voil

van	while	check	chap	slim
vane	whale	chick	chop	slime
vine	wheel	cheek	cheap	slam
vain	whirl	choke	chirp	slum

flit	sleep	steal	drape	braid
flat	slope	stile	drop	bread
fleet	slip	stole	drip	breed
float	slap	stool	droop	bride

not	cool	fat	got	hat
net	coal	fit	goat	hate
nut	call	fate	get	heat
neat	cull	feet	gut	hoot
note	cowl	foot	gate	hurt
nit	coil	feat	gout	halt

fan	gull	lit	Sam	sun
fin	gale	let	same	sin
fine	goal	lot	seem	seen
fern	gill	late	sum	soon
fun	gull	loot	seam	sane

sell	sat	tack	tame	Ben
still	seat	tick	time	bin
sale	sit	tock	Tim	bone
sail	set	tuck	Tom	barn
sole	site	take	team	born
soil	salt	took	term	bean

rod	mat	tell	lack	pack
rode	mate	tile	lick	peck
red	meet	tale	lock	pick
rid	mitt	tool	luck	pock
ride	meat	tail	leak	puck
raid	mute	toil	lake	peek
read	moat	till	lark	perk
road	mart	tool	like	pork
rood	met	toll	look	pike

cat	can	doll	dad	mile
cot	cane	dole	dead	mill
cute	con	deal	deed	mail
cut	cone	dell	died	mull
cote	coon	dull	did	male
cart	coin	dale	dud	meal
coat	corn	dill	dude	mule

man	rat	sack	will	shin
men	rate	sick	will	shin
mean	rite	sock	well	sheen
morn	rut	suck	wail	shone
moan	root	sake	weal	shun
main	rote	seek	wool	shorn
moon	rout	soak	wile	shan

fall	lad	pale	pan	pat
fail	led	pal	pain	pet
feel	laid	pail	pen	pit
fill	lid	peel	pin	pot
fell	lead	pole	pine	part
file	load	peal	pane	port
fool	lied	pile	pun	pert
fowl	loud	pool	pawn	pout

farm	jug	kit	map	quail
firm	jog	kite	mop	quell
fame	jig	Kate	mope	quill

sham	ding	clip	trip	slick
shame	dong	clap	trap	slack

sing	Dan	peach
sang	den	pitch
song	din	patch
sung	dine	porch
shed	shack	drink
shade	shake	drank
shop	shark	drunk
white	wheel	tread
whit	while	trade
sheet	whale	tried
whet	whirl	trod

cling	black	sprang	strap
clang	bleak	spring	strip
clung	block	sprung	stripe
straight	thrash	swim	snap
street	thresh	swam	snip
strut	thrush	swum	snipe
shall	shot	crack	treat
shell	short	creek	trait
shawl	shoot	crook	trout
scrap	creed	flip	Spain
scrape	cried	flap	spoon
scrip	crowd	flop	spine

Made in the USA
Lexington, KY
14 March 2017